A

LIGHT BULB

SYMPHONY

POEMS BY

PHIL KAYE

TABLE OF CONTENTS

TEETH

Ojichama is what I call my Japanese grandfather.
In 1945, his Tokyo home was burned to the ground.

Grampy is what I call my American grandfather.
In 1945, he was serving on the aircraft carrier USS Shangri-La,
sending off American fighter pilots to burn down Japanese houses.

Our jaws have not yet healed.

1906—Poland.
Grampy's father is hiding in an oven.
He has heard men singing on the street below.
Hyenas my family calls them.
After beers and song,
the townspeople come in to the Jewish ghetto
for a celebration beating—
molar fireworks and eyelid explosions.
Even when Grampy's father grows up
the sound of jubilant song
breaks his body into a sweat.

Fear of joy
is the darkest of captivities.

1975—Tokyo.
My father, the long-winded student
with a penchant for sexual innuendo,
meets Reiko Hori,

a well dressed banker
who forgets the choruses of her favorite songs.
Twelve years later they give birth
to a lanky light bulb.

1999—California.
My mother speaks to me in Japanese—
most days I don't have the strength to ask her to translate the big words.
We burned that house down Mother, don't you remember?

1771—Prague.
In the heart of the city, there is a Jewish cemetery—
the only plot of land
where Grampy's ancestors were permitted to be buried.
When they ran out of room, there was no choice
but to stack dead bodies one on top of the other.
Now the cemetery has hills
made from graves piled 12 deep,
individual tombstones jutting out crooked,
like valiant teeth
emerging from a jaw
left to rot.

1985—My parents wedding.
The two families sit together
smiling wider than they need to.
Montague must be so happy,
we can Capulet this all go.

1998—In the quiet of his Tokyo study,
Ojichama writes letters
addressed to his old four poster bed
on the backs of Betty Page postcards.
Haven't had a good night sleep
since the night you left.
Wish you were here.

2003—I sit with Grampy's cousin,
91 years old and dressed in full uniform.
I plead with him to untie the knots in his brow.
He says
Hate is a strong word,
but it is the only strength I have left.
How am I to forgive the men
that severed the trunk of my family tree
and used its timber to warm the cheeks
of their own children?

2009—Grampy and I
sit in silence
watching his favorite:
baseball.
I look over,
the infertile glare of the television reflects his face, wet.
Grampy sits in his wheelchair,
teeth gasping out of his gums
like valiant tombstones

emerging from a cemetery
left to rot.

The teeth sit staring,
and I can read them.
Louis Bergman, killed at Auschwitz.
Samantha Cohen, killed at Dachau.
William Cain, killed off the coast of Okinawa.

My voice rushes from the safety of its throat,
I will not forget what has happened to us, Grampy.

And he looks at me with the innocent surprise
of a child struck for the first time.

Philip,
Forgetting is the only gift I wish I to give you.
I have given away my only son
trying to bury my hate in a cemetary that is already overflowing.
There are nights I am kept awake
by the birthday songs of children
I never let live.

They often look like you.

A plague on both your houses
They have made worm's meat of me.

RACCOON MAN

Jonathan clings to my leg
with eyes like big bruised green apples.

"Phil," he says, "don't make me go home."
I have given Jonathan three weeks.
He has given me his life.

On our third day together,
Jonathan asks me how many push-ups I can do.
Not many.
He says, "Well I can do thirty-one push-ups,
which is probably more push-ups than you can do,
but I promise not to embarrass you if we are in front of girls."

He doesn't.
Jonathan has never lied to me,
although some days he gets close—
like after I tell him that a picture is worth a thousands words,
and for his first two-page essay
he hands me three-fourths of a Polaroid.

He has a way of laughing at things that scare me—
On costume day, Jonathan leaves the bruises under his eyes
and dresses up like a raccoon.

We laugh together outside one night—
A shooting star passes,
I tell him it's his to wish on.

He stops laughing,
tells me he doesn't do that any more.
Tells me that in eleven years
he has wished upon every star he can get his eyes on,
but they are too busy with quick fixes
like teddy bears and bicycles.

So I tell him to wish on the spaces between them

for it's the vacant places like that
that are just waiting to be called home.
And so he does.

The statistics say Jonathan won't make it.
And some days, Jonathan believes them.
He tells me that his father's bark is silent compared to the bite—
he can barely hear his own sobs over the bible versus his father recites
and as if I was Abraham himself, Jonathan holds me tight,
and together we try to learn how not to be scared to death,
but be scared to life.

Jonathan holds onto my leg like a mast on a sinking ship.
He says the spaces between stars have lied to him,
given him a three week home
and then ripped it away.
He is scared we will never speak again.
And I don't dare tell him the truth—
that when they first sent satellites between stars,

the sound of those fiery masses exploding was so violent
they thought the machine had imploded.

I pick Jonathan up from the floor and hold him to my chest.
He is sobbing so loudly he doesn't hear me weep.
Our chests pound against each other
like medics trying to shake each other to life.

And for the moment, I want to turn against every wry smile
that's ever harmed this little boy
and inflict the same fists that he has had to endure.

But Jonathan holds my fists tight under his chest.

And he knows I am no Abraham.
And quietly, I feel him slip through my arms, and shatter on the floor.
And there, like the countless pieces of an ornament
fallen off a last name too brittle to hold its weight,
Jonathan is falling through the cracks.

And desperately, with hands still red with blood
I pick up his pieces off the floor.
Jonathan, I cannot fix nor understand your life, but I will give you mine.

And on that sidewalk, holding hands,
we carefully place his shards piece by piece
until they take up the entire sky.
A magnificent mosaic—

a million tiny pictures,
worth a billion tiny words.
Words that we will speak back and forth
until the stars burn out
and our only home
will be the peaceful spaces between them.

Steadfastly holding onto our wishes,
patiently waiting to finally come true.

VIRGINITY

I was 11 years old when my dad first told me about vaginas.

It was a little early.

I had only just discovered my own genitalia.
Before that, my penis and I had been
awkward freshman year roommates—
we didn't spend much time with each other,
but we were polite enough.
I would get up to go the bathroom,
he would get up and stretch.

My dad didn't tell me as much about vaginas
as he did about his first time "making the love."
He was in high school,
she was his girlfriend,
and they both cut school that day.

At the end of the story, I asked my father,
who at the time I called *SuperPops*,
when I should first expect to "make the love."

"Oh I don't know, fifteen?"

Oh, I don't know, fiffuckingteen?

Thanks, Daddy Manslut.

◆

Fast Forward. Middle School.
Parker Thomson was half my height and twice as cool.
He was like the monkey from Aladdin,
if the monkey wore Dickies
and felt boobies like it was his job.
He told us around the lunch table,
"Scott Patterson's brother didn't have sex with his girlfriend
until he was 20.
He must be gay."

◆

Fast Forward.
Dear Diary,
sixteen looms on the horizon,
and I still haven't found anybody
that will have anything to do
with my nads.

I am doomed.

◆

Fast Forward.
16.

Nikki Babcock was a friend from Jewish camp.
And Nikki Babcock knew what she was doing.
The interaction went a bit like this:
"Hey Nikki, you look nice."
Make out make out make out
Nikki pulls back.
"Phil, I want to fuck your brains out."

It would be a full four hours until I lost my virginity that night.

After Nikki Babcock told me
she literally wanted to fornicate
until my cerebrum exploded,
I suggested we watch *The Land Before Time*.

But sitting watching that incredible film,
I had a powerful realization:
Nikki Babcock was going to show me her vagina.

I had an image of Vagina as some mysterious cloaked super being.
Like some awesome *Star Wars* character
that George Lucas saved until *Episode 7*,
when Han Solo finally dumps Princess Leia
to marry the most powerful Jedi of all time
Darth Punani.

Nikki Babcock and I finished the movie,
and went upstairs to my room.

Nikki stood in the corner,
took her clothes off herself,
and turned off the lights.

And just like that, I thought I had finally become my father's son.

♦

The next morning
I woke to the sound of the Ferguson's taking out the trash.
And that morning,
like every morning,
my dad and I sat in sleepy silence on the way to school.
I didn't know how to tell him about victory,
so after 10 minutes I finally asked,
"What do you remember most about your first time...having sex?"

He said what he remembers most
was the morning after—
waking up and feeling like he had
whispered some secret he never thought he'd be able to tell,
and having someone there to whisper it back.

He took a long pause,
and smiled to himself,
"Phil, someday
hopefully
you'll have the same morning."

THIS AMERICAN LIFE

Bye-bye Miss American Pie
Drove my Chevy to the levy
But the levy was broke
And good ol' boys
Drinking whiskey, smoking coke
Singing this'll be the day that I die
This will be the day that I die

And on the ninety billionth day God created radio
And last night I was suspended between Day One
and that place that clocks whisper about but don't dare go
My understanding hanging between Saturn Ring antennas
and a Milky Way dial
listening quietly to DJ Uncle Sam
Listening
Listening

This land is my land
This land is my land
From Guatemala to Hawaii
From Panama to the entire continent of Africa
This land was made for me to take

I lay and listened to him
and in that chilling emptiness
even without pupils
my eye sockets
could hear you all there

I heard our childhood sympathies
banging against each other in a giant communal eardrum circle
trying to drown out melodies we can't help but hum to
because DJ Uncle Sam has been playing worldwide
his shit has been on top since, like, 1945

We're bringing imperial back (Yeah!)
Them other countries don't know how to act (Yeah!)
But we'll make sure that we tell them that (Yeah!)
Britain come over and pick up the slack (Yeah!)
Take 'em to the

Bridges collapsing onto my back and I awake on my knees begging
calling in to the cosmic station
trying to get a hold of that DJ that started it all
The One who can remix relevances into a Renaissance of perfect being
I can remember his warmth but never his name
DJ Allah or DJ Shen or DJ J.C.?
Somebody told me he just goes by DJ Clockmaker
that he just spins the record and lets us scratch it up
But if only he'd change the song
because I just want something I can dance to

But instead I
Change the station
Institutional genocide
Change the station
Overfilled prisons

Change the station
Broken school system
Change the station
Institutionalized racism
Change the station
Crank out more soldia boys and then drop 'em like they hot

Oh yeah that's the good shit!
Play that over and over and over
and people will still
Lean with it
Vote for it
Lean with it
Vote for it

Dig boys, Dig!
It's just desert soil!
Holes in the sand are good for graves
and for oil

Last night I found my radio awake
with eyes wide
eyes red
singing our song
Gimme gimme more
Gimme more
Gimme gimme

I ache for days when radio sounded like politics and not the opposite
Fireside chats not side chats in this inferno

Last night I heard my country singing songs like crooks
not singing choruses but singing hooks
leaders roasting compromise over burning history books
I was searching for our justice, but I didn't know where to look

And I can't find it anywhere in this radio so I keep digging
And I can't find it anywhere in my veins so I keep digging
And there never seems to be enough oil or enough graves
so I keep digging

I'll keep digging until my arms disappear
then I'll dig with my throat
I'll keep digging until its just my toes
just enough to turn this up before I go

♦

You know what's a fun game?
You listen to a song real tender and real slow
And sometimes it will whisper the secrets it promised to keep
But I've got a shovel sitting outside
and a wide-eyed conscience ready to play seek-and-hide
so we'll just do one before I go

♦

Land where my fathers died

Chinese Exclusion Act
1790 Naturalization Act
Jim Crow Laws

Land of the pilgrims' pride

Indian Removal Act
Literacy Tests
1907 Gentleman's Agreement

From every mountainside

Alien and Sedition Acts
Smallpox blankets
1934 National Housing Act
Dred Scott v. Sandford
The Cross Bronx Expressway
Japanese internment

Let freedom ring

JESUS WILL DO IT FOR HALF

When my best friend goes on dates,
men take her to rooftops
or motorcycle back seats.

I take girls to Starbucks—
because I can never recognize the music
in independent coffee houses.

But starting today,
I have made a commitment to be more exciting.

I will go to Disneyland
and say hello to Mickey Mouse
while dressed as a giant mousetrap.

I will start to do things like
go into public bathroom stalls
and write notes on the toilet paper:
I BEG YOU SIR, DON'T SUFFOCATE ME IN YOUR POOP!

I will do clever things like
go to my Rabbi and ask for a refund
because Jesus has given me a better offer.

I will go to McDonald's
and respond,
"I'm lovin' it!"
to everything the cashier says.

Dear girl that-have-not-met-yet-but-hopefully-will-in-the-near-
future:
We will be so happy together
that you will call and tell your friends things like,
"I feel like a Care Bear. ON ECSTACY."

Someone in passing will say,
"I love this restaurant,
I've come like six times."
And I will quip, "That's what she said!"
and you actually will.

Now when I go on dates
I will have to wear a long sleeve shirt
to cover up my life-size uber-realistic tattoo
of a short sleeve shirt.

When we skinny dip in the river,
I will give away our clothes
so we must race to warm hum of my room
under our fort of bed sheets and breath.

And when we finally say goodbye,
I will not be the only one
standing quietly behind the closed door
hoping for it to swing open again.

Now
I am very confident
that none of this will happen.
Because my relationship with my Rabbi is quite strong.
And the cape of spontaneity
has always felt tight around my shoulders.

But some days
you just desperately need someone to tell you

this
all feels brand new.

SHE ASKS ME

Wide eyed she asks me,
"What *is* Spoken Word?
I mean—Isn't that what I just heard
on the radio, a minute ago
and turned up the volume to get a little crescendo?
When my system was bumping
my friends were jumping
and Fifty was talking about pumping,
some lead into some dude with his berretta
just so he can betta his sickest vendetta?
And who are you, *Phil Kaye*—
because I just hate to say,
but you look a couple shades too pale
to sound like the songs that sing about
being out on bail, fresh out of jail, California Dreamin'
and more more more
with the Escalade on rims with the Lamborghini doors."

And I said to her that *that*
is true.

Because my sole is void of holes
and my soul is void of the scars
you get from being behind bars
or from waking up and feeling that no matter how wise you are
you will always be marginalized by society's eyes.

So no, I was not raised on the streets—
but if you strip away those instrumental beats
and the platinum teeth
and ego
all you are left with
are words.

And all spoken word poetry is,
is words arranged to try to propagate change
or spread love
or just open the mind.

And if you press rewind on the timeline you'll find
that *this* is nothing edgy or new or underground.
It can be found in the sound of Mahatma Gandhi's voice,
drowned by the sound of cheers
calling for someone
with powerful ears to listen after all these years.
It can be found in the whisper of your mother
reading you bedtime stories when you were afraid to fall asleep alone.
It can be found everyday when he realizes he is actually in love,
his words become doves
no stops to speak of,
just thinking,
Damn, we fit like a glove.

Poetry is eternity,
and we're just specks you see

dabbling in its mystery
transcending history
and I once was blind
but now can
write.

So no, I was not raised on the streets—
but neither was poetry.
It woke up with the first sunrise
opened with the first eyes
gave birth to dragonflies
comforted baby cries
and cursed me with my eyes.

My eyes that see a world obsessed with the *us and them*
the flowers and stems, where Black and Tans brutalize
blackened hands.
And I don't understand because poetry is produced
by the cerebrum which is pink
and the vocal chords which are red
and if we spelled out our poems in blood
no one would care what color they came from.

So this is me
right now
not knowing how I'm going to get through the next fifteen seconds.
My future, it beckons, and I'm not quite ready to reckon with it yet.
All I have is my soul, and someone told me that that is poetry.

So when I'm dead in the ground,
my soul six feet down,
my tombstone will read for some child to see
and smile when she's done:

Here Lies a Man's Private Poetry
Trespassers Welcome

FUNERALS ARE LIKE BIRTHDAY PARTIES

Miriam sings sticky under the sheets
and stares up through the ceiling.
We sit in an empty neon hospital
like an aborted Easter egg
forgotten long past April.

She says that funerals are like birthday parties
except better.
No one wastes money on presents,
and everyone dresses up for the theme.

Miriam has been waiting to go for eight months now.
Today she stands tall on the dock,
her bags neatly packed.

Smile,
she says.
Lives are meant to be spent,
now I am in debt,
and I am tired of borrowing from the people I love.

For my party,
put me in a nice dress,
no straps.
I have very nice shoulders.
She laughs.

No Priest.
No Roses.
No Guns.

She wants everyone to bring a bouquet of sunflowers
and then find someone else to give them to.

For a band,
She wants every secret shower singer,
every three-chord bedroom rock star,
every sore-thigh drummer—
a light bulb symphony.

She sighs and lets go of my hand.
As she walks up to the boat, she smiles back and waves to us
as if to say,
Don't worry, I will write.

And carefully, so as to not ruin her hair,
Miriam places the elastic strap of her birthday hat around her chin.
And disappears through the doorway.

HIP HOP LULLABY

Dear Nas,
Where does Hip Hop go when it dies?
Is it all just maggots and flies
or will Hip Hop rise and come again?
Come again?
Jay-Z back again with Beyonce and 'em—
that seems alive.

Are you dispensing wisdom
because I want to listen,
or are you just throwing out
this and that,
verbal tit for tat,
mixing fiction and fact—
will Hip Hop fade to black
or merely rot to rap, hmm?

And who killed Hip Hop?
Because I heard he suffocated in a CD case—
mass-marketed, 106 and Parketed, Sprite sponsorshipped.

Or was it Jacob the Jeweler?
No dude was ever cooler,
Hip Hop—out of G's he fooled you,
got you buying
platinum nooses,
throwbacks to white abuses—
useless.

Or was it the Romans and Pontius Pilot?
Got his panties in a bunch and got violent,
rolled up his sleeves and got physical
because with crosses, resurrections, and *God's Son* albums
this shit has become biblical.

Or was it me?
Did I kick Hip Hop
when it was sick didn't stop
till it was shit fused pop,
till it was blue in the face,
or white in the face—

Or was it me?
Because I know at Hip Hop's birth
the room smelled thick of dark chocolate,
and decades later my white frosting might be ruining the recipe.
Me—pretending the Teflon,
ghostriding the Nissan,
trying to put a few pounds on
so I can fill out the Sean Jean.

Because this death plays like a detective movie
with Hip Hop lying in a pool of blood, deceased,
and then the camera pans up and there stands me
standing over, with the smoking barrel of my wallet.
You see, Nas, I agree with you—
Hip Hop is dead,

but he's bred daughters and sons,
rappers trying climb to number one
singing the same new song of misogyny and guns,
spitting in the face of their fathers: Public Enemy, KRS-1.

Hip Hop is dead,
but he's bred daughters and sons,
a generation of little faces being taught to shun
peace, humility, and education
when in California they estimate the number of jail cells to build
by the number of forth graders who can't read.

Hip Hop is dead,
but he's bred sons and daughters,
and "I ain't a playa I just fuck a lot" doesn't leave room for fathers,
and Hip Hop's buying cars, Cristal, and shit to snort,
but Brenda's still got a baby that she didn't abort,
and Hip Hop's not been known to pay his child support.

So forget Mick Jagger, Papa, or that goddamn magazine,
Hip Hop was the original rolling stone.
Traveling across the country,
fucking kids consensually,
and essentially, leaving them alone,
and eventually, leading them to unknown,
and essentially, stripping me down to this poem.
And I'm not standing here trying to show them
that Hip Hop isn't beautiful

because it is.
Hip Hop is power,
but when did clenched fists
relax to just this?

So if you're there Hip Hop,
this is a prayer Hip Hop—

you may have died for our sins,
but please come back
because once again
we are ready
to begin.

AYEKAYE
FOR AURORA

It takes a tremendous amount of love
to call someone while you're pooping.

You called me yesterday from our favorite sandwich place.
Called to tell me how good it smelled,
and your ensuing amazement over the absence of potpourri.
"It must just be me," you said.

It's days like this I wonder what I'm doing
3,000 miles away from the only person
whose skipping stone heart
leaves ripples that sound just like mine
when they lap against the shore—

how you and I
filled up the six years that separates us
with memories rank with unconditional love.

Sitting in silence licking envelopes for Sharon Wolf.
Getting lost for two hours in the paper lantern section of IKEA.
Deciding which Jonas Brothers poster to buy from Claire's.

I keep all your cards
like Magic Marker prayers.
I hang them up around my days
like Post-it notes that read, "Live."
Because you made me believe in ice cream for dinner.
And Disneyland on a school day.

And Mom.

At dinner tables you fall quiet like curtains,
as if our lives grabbed for the same wishbone
and you walked away with the smaller half.
But don't believe it.
I'm not flying—
I've just tried too hard to hide the wires.

Some days you've got a slingshot for a mouth.
Those days jump on my shoulders,
and we'll take down our Goliaths.

Some days I watch you crumble like a sandcastle.
Those days let me climb over your gates
and rebuild you out of brick.

And some days the creases in your fingers
are the closest thing I have to forgiveness.
And those days take me with you.

And those nights when my skinny arms were too weak
to hold up our heavy home,
you made the name Big Brother sound like a superhero.

And after 16 years of electric laughter in 40-watt rooms,
and doors slammed so softly we lost our breath—
I find myself here

with too many rivers and too few sailboats between us.

So stretch out across me
like Blue Key to Thayer Street,
like kids eat free to senior citizen discount,
like this life is just the opening credits.

I wish I could be there to watch you grow
into something even more extraordinary
than the you you've already become

But I'm left with faded flower pedal photographs,
and my ear to the soil,
listening to rumbles you're making halfway around the world—

so the nights I need you most
I take a pocket full of skipping stones
And off the New York coast
I listen to you breathe.

And just so you know,
In the future
you don't need to call me
from the bathroom,
startled by your own brand of remarkable.
I've known for years
it must just be you.

SUBURBIA

I love this place.
The people,
the community,
the sense of stability.

This place is amazing.
This place is amazing!
This place
is a maze
is a maze
is a maze

♦

The Law of Conservation states that
energy can not be created or destroyed,
only transformed from one state to another.
1945—Albert Einstein, a man of law, helps create the atomic bomb.
100,000 Japanese houses implode, American Surburbia explodes.

♦

Read the paper! We're choking! The City, she's been smoking!
There is her body: wrinkled, cracking, loose.

Out there on the fringe—there is plenty,
space so empty you can stretch your arms out inside of her.
Thick. Overgrown.

That's how you know she's a virgin.

♦

1970—
This is the 20th century!
We knew we'd reach the Pacific eventually,
this is just our new Manifest Destiny.

By this time the number of Americans
living in the suburbs
has exploded by 300 percent.

Locusts / Hocus / Pocus / Poof!
Smoke makes you choke,
but at least
it is air.

♦

City? City. City?

♦

City has woken up mid-surgery.
The suitcase of her chest ripped open.
Her skyscraper intestines pulled out and put down sideways.
She calls for help:

Nurse! Give me more anesthesia!
I was never truly sleeping,
only for a moment American dreaming.

♦

The nurse with the rag to our face:

Breathe! Everyone is happy!

Our little American sequel,
seagulls, regal, fecal, illegal,
impossible, separate, equal!

Popular real estate textbooks
highlight the importance of social homogeneity.

♦

The thing about weeds, Mr. Kennedy,
is their penchant for multiplying.
You let just one in your community,
and sooner or later
you'll find one in your very own backyard.
Well then—there goes the neighborhood.
There goes the neighborhood.

♦

Go. Go. Farther.
Outside of the garden.
City on a sill—oops had a little spill!
Looked like an accident, wouldn't quite call it kill.
I'm choking! City's been smoking!
Give me throatdrops! Or is it Winthrops?
City on a pill!

Go. Go. Farther.
Our little mazes, mousetraps, cul-de-sacs,
This house is amazing!
This house is amazing!
This house is amazing!
This house is amazing!
This house is amazing!

Farther! Farther!
Father,
raise me, graze me, open range me, open flame me—
We are all not the same, are we? *Are we?*

Run
eat
water
food
fence
water
fence

eat
run
fence
water
food
fence

♦

Shhh.

Breathe.

Everyone is happy.

You're only making this more difficult
for yourself.

FOR TREY

The funny thing about dead people
is that you cannot feel
when they crawl into bed with you.

His stubble scratched against my eyes
as he whispered into my ear:

You start to think
about a lot of things
before you do it.

He said it started because the light
at the end of the tunnel
was only getting father away,
and so he was finally turning things around
and was going to get there now.

But he said that at the silence of the ledge,
he could distinctly hear his father
cheering after his first basket.

He said you remember entire afternoons
you forced yourself to forget
because the daylight emanating from the finger-worn edges
made today too hard.

He said that logic drips away
with wrongs and rights and words and fights,

and the handprint of every woman he ever held was burned into his skin,
and as he screamed
the vastness stole away his voice
like a common pickpocket.

He said that the movies are a lie—
you don't see it flash before your eyes,
instead you dance whole-body in a swimming pool
filled with that one night you couldn't stop laughing
and the first CD you ever bought is blaring in the foreground.

He said that entire love affairs get balled up
into one fleeting instant,
like a caramel that tastes
like the small of her back.

The oddest part are your toes.
As they curl over the edge
you become sure that standing upright
was just Heaven's old wives tale,
and gravity was favored to win anyway.
And when you lean forward and look
at the gorgeous scene below
you finally remember that it's just a page in a storybook—
and you know the story,
but can't remember any of the words,
and you're finally ready to be part of the pages.

And in seconds that looked like days,
he rummaged through memorized equations
and phone numbers that never picked up
and found a box of unanswered birthday cake wishes—
and he poured them over the edge
and watched them glitter in the sun like paper airplanes.
He swore could catch them.

He promised right then that all the wretched love
that had been starved from him
would manifest itself into two magnificent wings.
Wings that would envelope continents and decades and her eyelashes
and would carry him away to another storybook
filled with pretty pictures and a happy ending.

He said his hands had always been too small to have long lifelines,
and today he would find other palms to forget them in.

He said that history has a way of forgetting
those that followed the rules,
and this was his silent revolution.
Because the tanks had all gone home,
and the armbands had become fashion,
and revolution was nothing but a t-shirt.

But today he would spring himself free,
like the first note of fresh saxophone—
and every being would laugh and smile

because the funny thing about dead people
is that you don't know they're there
until they're not.

And he held me tight.
He held me sharp.
He held me like he finally understood that his wings
were sublime, and gorgeous,
and heavy.

And that morning,
the stain of pillow tears looked like his face,
and for the first time in my life
I prayed—

that knobby fingers could become feathers,
and gaunt spines could inhale with the wind,
and that somewhere in the distance
a boy was resting—
a pile of paper planes at his feet.

ACKNOWLEDGEMENTS

Thank you
To all my family
Whether or not we share a last name
You know who you are

This collection would not have been possible without
Steve Daniels, Sarah Kay & the WORD! family

ABOUT THE AUTHOR

Phil Kaye has been writing, performing and teaching Spoken Word Poetry since he was seventeen years old. A Brown University graduate now based in New York City, Phil has been a semifinalist at both the National Poetry Slam and the College National Poetry Slam (CUPSI) where he was awarded for "Pushing the Art Forward." He is the co-director of Project V.O.I.C.E. and travels across the country performing his work and teaching Spoken Word workshops with his poetry partner-in-crime, Sarah Kay.

For more information, video footage, and booking details:
www.project-voice.net
philip.kaye@gmail.com

Printing by Blurb.

Made in the USA
Middletown, DE
09 December 2018